#JesusTherapy andMeds

by
TJ Ogunlusi

ISBN: 978-0-578-74803-0

#JesusTherapyandMeds

Proudly self-published through Divine Legacy Publishing, www.divinelegacypublishing.com

Dedication

In loving memory of Donnell Corbett, Sr. (August 14, 1966 - November 11, 2011) and Priscilla Lynn Corbett (October 11, 1973 - March 29, 2013).

Forward

Here I was six months pregnant, feeling completely anxious about my upcoming postpartum experience. I'd just left my doctor's appointment where she briefed me on her concerns about my history with depression and anxiety. I'm mostly a "suffer in silence" kind of girl. I get easily offended by others' input about my mental health. To drown my sorrows, I began to scroll through social media. There I saw the bold, courageous, and incredibly vulnerable T.J. sharing her struggles with the world. She expressed herself with such transparency, confidence, and conviction. I felt compelled to reach out. I'd been where she was in postpartum. I knew all too well what she was going through. The difference between her and I was that she was open. T.J. and I have known each other for years, but in this experience a connection was born.

T.J. and I spent the next few months helping each other cope and process what was happening within us and our bodies. We spent many times on our knees on behalf of each other praying for deliverance. I would share my postpartum experience from my first child with her, things I had never shared with anyone before. It was uncanny how similar our stories were. Jesus, therapy, and medication were our saving graces. T.J., being the advocate, decided that women needed to know they weren't alone. Not everyone is going to be as fortunate to find a kindred spirit who is willing to keep it real and transparent. She decided to step up, lean in, and pour her heart out for the world to see.

#JesusTherapyandMeds was born. #JesusTherapyandMeds is an intimate look at a strong woman's personal journey toward mental healing. A woman, like you and me, who is capable, strong, and intelligent being brought to her knees by this process. It's a riveting memoir filled with trauma, triggers, prayer, and healing. It will be transforming to us all. As moms, our silent cries will finally be put into words. We will finally feel understood. With this book, a sisterhood will be born. We will be able to read this book and share this sense of knowing with one another. That "knowing" will be the gift of togetherness. If you've never experienced postpartum or other mental health challenges, this book will give you empathy and sensitivity to those in your life who have. It will give you a glimpse of battles you've never experienced. This book is for every woman who has ever had a personal battle that could only be won with the power of Jesus and the resource of therapy. #Jesustherapyandmeds is a must read for all.

With Love,
Carina Marie

The Trauma

"Tash, stop! Please stop! Stopppp!"

My mother's cries of pain and distress often rang in my ears growing up; physical, mental, and emotional abuse were no strangers in my home. My mother met my father in Camden, New Jersey in the late 80s. She was just fifteen years old. He was twenty-three. Shortly after meeting, my mother became pregnant with me. From what I can remember of her from back then, she was smart. She was strong. She was ambitious. She had her own identity. However, becoming a teen mother forced her to give up any dreams and aspirations she may have had, and she quickly settled into the role of a submissive teen mom and high-school dropout with an abusive baby daddy.

My father was an alcoholic for as far back as I can remember. He drank from sunup to sundown. He stumbled around the neighborhood drunk and slurring his speech. During one drunken binge, he was hit with a two by four, which resulted in permanent nerve damage in his face. Alcohol was the gasoline that fueled the eruption of abuse that rained on my mother's body and waged war on her mind. She was kicked, punched, slapped, and God knows what else. She was cursed out...called a bitch...called a hoe...anything but the name her mother gave her and a child of God. She was accused of cheating with coworkers and was forced to quit working for good as a result. One explosive night in particular led to her pinky being broken. I couldn't have been more than six at the time, but I remember that night. And so, this was the cycle of abuse that would replay over and over for years to come and eventually manifest into the physical and mental abuse of my sister and myself.

The abuse that my mother endured at the hands of my father slowed down once he stopped drinking cold turkey. It was the mid 90s and my father had asked my mother to marry him several times. By this time, they had added two additional children to the mix, my brother Jamal and my sister Gwendolyn. Though my mother would go on to have a total of four children before they eventually wed in 1997, she refused to marry him without an ultimatum: Stop drinking. So he did. They had a courthouse wedding on August 14, 1997, my dad's birthday. I fed my new baby sister, Sasha, as they exchanged their vows. And just like that, we were a "real" family.

The physical aspects of the abuse dwindled once my dad stopped drinking, but the mental and emotional aspects ramped up. During the next several years, my father was the only one who worked. Though my mother no longer worked outside of the home, it did not stop my father from accusing her of cheating. I remember one particular incident vividly. We had moved to North Carolina in 2000 because my mother wanted a fresh start. I was not pleased. North Carolina was hot and the water at my great grandmother's house tasted like eggs. Plus, who wanted to live in the country with a bunch of dirt roads? I had firsthand knowledge of this because we had visited my dad's family a few times in the previous years. But, a ten year old does not have a say in such matters, so off we all went.

One Saturday afternoon, we went out to support my brother as he competed in the Special Olympics. Apparently, during the competition, one of the male teen volunteers was "looking" at my mom. Now, none of us knew for sure if this had indeed happened, but my dad insisted that it did. Despite her having absolutely no control over who was or was not "looking" at her, my mother was blamed. My father started an argument in public. I was embarrassed and ashamed as he cursed her out. Again, she was a bitch...she was a hoe...she was a cheater...she wanted this teenager. Of course, none of this made any sense. But to my father, it had to be true. He had my mother right where he wanted her, at least for now.

Not long after we moved to North Carolina, my dad started having problems with his back. He had worked with a moving company for several years before we moved. This hard labor ruined him. The next few years consisted of several back surgeries, infections, and a deadly opioid addiction that he would never kick.

Watching my father high on painkillers was like Deja vu. He stumbled around the house. His speech was slurred. He dropped lit cigarettes. He drove under the influence. He ran into a ditch with me in the car. He almost hit a school bus. He caused us to almost be hit head on by a truck. All while under the influence. Watching and taking care of him became my new normal.

Watching and taking care of my siblings also became second nature to me during this time. On one such occasion, when I was sixteen, I came home from school to find both of my parents missing. The only clue was a half-eaten meatball sub lying in my parent's room. Naturally, I was terrified, but I could not show my fears because I had four kids to look after. So, we waited. And waited. And waited. At around 10 pm that night, there was a knock at the door. It was Child Protective Services. Apparently, my father was in the hospital after falling asleep at the wheel and almost hitting a school bus. My mother was in jail for writing a bad check. She would be out the next morning, but nobody knew that at the time. So, off we went. The five of us were split up. Gwendolyn and Jamal were sent to one home while Sasha and Natalie were sent to another. I was alone.

We spent a total of two weeks in foster care. That may not seem like a long time, but it was excruciating. The homes we were in were not terrible; we all were lucky enough to be with families who cared. However, this was not what I was accustomed to. It seemed like my life had been shaken up overnight. I was separated from my parents and siblings with the blink of an eye. My life at home may not have been ideal, but at the time, it was familiar. Thankfully, the two weeks ended, and we were all reunited again. But that reunion was short lived.

My mother had decided that she'd had enough. During one of my after school band practices, I received a phone call. It was my mother. She had decided that she could no longer take my dad's addiction and that she was moving to Georgia and taking my two baby sisters with her. I had no say so. Her tone was very matter of fact. Up until this point, my sympathy and loyalty was with my mother. However, that all changed the day she left. Yes, my dad was an addict. But in my mind, it was not his fault. He had been dealt a tough hand. My mother was now the enemy for abandoning him and us, and I hated her. It would take years and therapy for me to understand her side and empathize with her.

My mother did not stay in Georgia for too long. Six months later, she was back and I was pissed. How dare she leave us and then pop back up trying to regulate? In my mind, I was the head of the household. I cooked. I cleaned. I took care of my father. I took care of the brother and sister who were also left behind. And here she was, back and trying to discipline me. I was not having it. And so, the cycle of her abuse toward me began.

Before my mother left, her physical and verbal abuse was directed toward my sister Gwendolyn. It was a vicious cycle. My mother would get beaten and cursed out by my father and she would then turn on my sister. Once she returned from Georgia, her abuse became directed toward me. Granted, I did have a smart mouth and a huge issue with her telling me what to do, but the abuse messed me up mentally. Every time my mother would hit me, slap me, pull my hair, and tell me that she hated me, I would feel worthless. I believed every word that she said to me. One time, the pastor of our church came over to mediate one of the many conflicts my mother and I were getting into. He made us hug and during that embrace, my mother whispered that she hated me in my ear. I could not believe it. It seemed that nobody could intervene and make my mother see reason and what she said to me had to be true.

This pain was what led to me to start cutting myself. In my mind, cutting was my way of punishing myself for being everything that my mother said that I was. I would sit in my room after one of her verbal or physical attacks and break light bulbs. I used the sharp edges of the bulbs to cut myself deep enough to bleed. I was smart enough to make sure the cuts were in places that could not be easily seen. My arms. My legs. My stomach. There was one person I hoped who would notice. I wanted my mother to see the pain that she was causing me, but she either didn't notice or chose to ignore the signs. She walked in my bedroom in the midst of me bleeding one day and did not say a word. It was at that moment that I knew my only means of escape was through education. And so I threw myself into my studies.

For as long as I can remember, the importance of school was drilled into me. I was taught that B's were unacceptable and was even beaten for getting two C's on my progress report in middle school. I learned a hard lesson early. By this time, both parents were on disability, so there was no way that I was going to be able to pay for school unless I got a scholarship. And so I pushed myself. I studied and competed with my white classmates. I spent every summer at Upward Bound Math and Science camp at Western Carolina University conducting and presenting academic research. I took college classes my junior and senior years, which allowed me to graduate undergrad a year early. It was important to me to be better than my white counterparts. Many of them had rich parents who could pay for their schooling out of pocket. My hard work and dedication paid off. I was awarded a full ride to Claflin University and entered the class of 2012 in 2008. I was finally free. However, that freedom was short lived because I still had ties to back home.

I tried to enjoy college as much as I could and, for the most part, it was an amazing experience. I was lucky enough to meet my college room-mates/suitemates who are some of my best friends to this day. But I still felt this nagging guilt in the back of my mind. By 2009 my mother had moved back to Georgia with my sisters, Sasha and Natalie. My brother, Jamal, and sister, Gwendolyn, were with my dad. I would get multiple phone calls about my dad being under the influence. Every time I received a call, I would feel this guilt. It broke my heart to know that my dad was home, virtually alone and I, his primary caretaker at that point, was off at school. This led me to spend Christmas and summers with my father instead of my mom. By the end of 2009, my brother and sister had had enough of my dad's addiction and had gone to live with a friend from church and her family. I was livid with them both. I felt a sense of responsibility for my father and felt that it was my job to take care of him. Anyone who had "abandoned" my father was the enemy in my eyes. That included my mother and now my brother and sister. So, I came home to him that Christmas. It was just me and my dad that year. I cooked and cleaned for him and watched sitcoms with him all day.

By the end of that trip home, my dad had decided that it would be better for him to move back to New Jersey to be closer to family. I felt better about going back to school because he would be around my grandmother and his brother. I thought that would be best for him and that maybe he would attend rehab in order to kick his drug addiction.

I was wrong.

On November 10, 2011, I received the last phone call I would ever receive from my dad. He was calling to tell me that he loved me. Of course, I didn't think anything of it. It was a normal interaction. However, that next morning, I received the worst possible news. I was in my apartment getting ready when my boyfriend at the time called and told me he was coming over. My grandmother could never remember my phone numbers and could only find my boyfriend's. He came to my room and handed me his phone. It was a voicemail from my grandmother. My father was dead. I immediately burst into tears. My heart was broken. This had been the first time I had experienced the death of a close family member. Perhaps one of the worst parts of all of this was that I had to be the one to call my mother and my siblings to break the news to them. Everyone's world was shattered, even my mother's.

We did not find out the cause of my father's death until months later. It was an accidental overdose. However, part of me still wonders if it was truly an accident. After all, he had called me and my siblings to tell us that he loved us just the night before. Did he take the pills on purpose? Was it my fault? Would things have turned out differently if I had not gone off to college? It was, after all, my responsibility to take care of my father, or at least I believed it was. I will never know the answer to any of those questions, but the guilt and weight of them still haunt me to this day.

My Family History of Mental Illness

Growing up, there was always a stigma surrounding someone who had a mental illness. That person was considered to be "crazy." The irony of this was that almost every person in my house suffered with some sort of mental illness. I grew up watching my mother, Gwendolyn, and Jamal see a psychiatrist and take medicine. I was not quite sure what my mother's diagnosis was at the time, but I knew that she took Klonopin on a regular basis. I later learned that this medication is a benzodiazepine prescribed for a multitude of anxiety disorders. It made sense that my mother was taking this medication considering the abuse she endured at the hands of my father. She probably suffered from PTSD as well.

Despite my mother's own challenges with mental health, it did not stop her from calling my sister crazy for her own mental health issues. It was strange. There seemed to be a tug of war of thoughts. Mental health issues meant you were crazy, but my mother was also an advocate of treatment, especially when it came to my sister. By the time she was ten years old, Gwendolyn had been diagnosed with Bipolar Disorder and Depression and had completed a stay at an inpatient treatment facility in Chapel Hill, North Carolina. I remember visiting her while she was there, and I also remember the doctor's warnings not to take her out of treatment too early. They warned my mother that if my sister did not remain in inpatient treatment longer, her issues would grow worse as she grew older. Of course, they were right. However, my mother wrestled with the guilt of my sister being so far away and our family not being able to visit her as often as she would have liked. And so, she checked her out of the facility. My sister would grow up to become resistant to both medication and treatment as a result.

Jamal's mental health challenges began a little earlier. He was diagnosed with ADHD and a mild form of retardation. This caused him to be in a self-contained classroom for a few years, and he repeated kindergarten a few times. As a result of his ADHD, he was prescribed Adderall. My father noticed that the medication caused my brother to slow down and "be good". He decided that it would be a great idea for all of the children to take the medication even though it was only prescribed to my brother and none of us were diagnosed with ADHD. So, every day around lunchtime, my dad would place the little blue pill in our mouths and then check to make sure we swallowed it. It tasted like candy and the cologne my dad wore. The medication made me lethargic and sick to my stomach. I would take a nap the same time each day and then wake up groggy. It was clear that we should not have been taking this medication, but it made all of the children in the house "be good."

Jamal's mental health challenges began to escalate the older he got. He would hallucinate and see things like bees with magic wands flying in the air. He saw his kindergarten graduation cap and gown flying around his room on their own. One time, he stuck his hand in a bowl of scalding soup because he thought that bugs were crawling all over it. We thought these episodes were funny as kids but the older we got, we began to grasp the seriousness of the issue. Things reached a breaking point for my brother when my dad passed away from his overdose. Nobody expected it; we were all blindsided. Jamal took things the hardest. He began to morph into a replica of my father. He would steal sleeping pills from the dollar store and pop multiples at a time, mixing them with alcohol and his prescription medications. It is a miracle that history did not repeat itself.

One night, Jamal had taken a bunch of pills and began foaming at the mouth. He started yelling and screaming that he was going to run in front of a truck. My mother and stepfather had to physically prevent him from leaving the house. They ended up calling an ambulance because my brother was grieving and suicidal. Once he was picked up, he was sent to an inpatient mental health facility in Villa Rica, Georgia. Being in the facility helped to stabilize him. It was there that he was diagnosed with schizophrenia. He was eighteen. So many things began to make sense. All of the hallucinations from his childhood made sense. We were now beginning to educate ourselves about his condition and the stigma about being "crazy" began to shift. My mother began to do all that she could to help my brother in his condition, including getting him more consistent appointments with a psychiatrist and having my younger sisters assist with medication management since he too had issues with addiction.

We found out that my paternal uncle also suffered from schizophrenia when we went to visit our family in New Jersey during the summer of 2017. He would talk to himself and people who were not there and have angry outbursts where he would yell and curse out anyone in his path. That included my oldest daughter. It was a scary and enlightening experience, especially because Jamal is now living with my grandmother and uncle. However, it allowed us to begin having conversations about mental health awareness with my daughter. Now when we visit, we are fully prepared for what we may see, and we know how to diffuse tough situations when they arise.

Of course, it was not just my uncle who suffered from mental health issues. I recently found out that my grandmother (my dad's mother) suffers from Panic Disorder. I was having a conversation with her about my recent diagnoses (Panic Disorder, GAD, and PTSD) and describing how I had just started having panic attacks after the birth of my second daughter. It was then that she opened up about her own experiences with Panic Disorder. She was very matter of fact when discussing her experience as she had become accustomed to it after many years. She told me that she was prescribed Buspar to combat the disorder, but that she did not like the way the medication made her feel. So, she deals with the disorder on her own. Despite spending a lot of time at my grandmother's house growing up and as an adult, I had no idea that she suffered with panic attacks until I opened up about my own struggles.

The older I got, the more I began to see that genetics played a role in everyone's challenges with mental health. We were predisposed to our conditions because members of both sides of the family also had these disorders. Yes, there were environmental factors that played a role as well. However, there was no mistaking that many of our challenges were because of genetics.

My Own Struggles with Mental Illness

Though my own struggles with mental illness went undiagnosed officially until I was 27 years old, it was clear that I too suffered from mental illness. I sank into a dark depression when my mother and I began having our issues when she returned back to our home in North Carolina. Between those issues and the weight of the responsibility of taking care of my addict father, I fell into a dark, dark place. I cut myself regularly to make someone, anyone, notice my pain. I cut to punish myself because, in my mind,

I deserved it. However, my mother didn't notice. Nobody did. So, I buried my feelings until they came bubbling to the surface years later. I had to bury them. How else was I going to function as a "normal" human being? There were still so many things to get done, including working hard to get a full ride to college so, away the feelings went. Or so I thought. Whenever I was asked about the source of my scars, I would lie and say that my dog did it or I would divert attention to another scar that was caused by my childhood recklessness. It was not until I was married that I told my husband the truth about those scars.

As an adult, I continued to struggle with mental health challenges, but I was no longer in that dark hole. The closest I came to being back in that place was after losing both of my parents unexpectedly, but even that did not cause me to cut. My mother passed about a year and a half after my father did on March 29, 2013. She was diagnosed with lung cancer at 39 and died a month later. I would have moments of situational moderate depression and though I did not know it at the time, my General Anxiety Disorder was alive and fully functioning way more than my depressive episodes.

As a child, all I did was worry. I would worry about my mother's safety and worry that my father would kill us in a car accident or burn our house down when high. I would worry that bad things would happen to people I cared about. This worry was amplified once both of my parents passed away unexpectedly. Now, I had new worries. I became obsessed with my own mortality, often having intrusive thoughts about when I would die. Would it be a car accident? Would I be murdered? Would I die of natural causes? Would my family be prepared? Would I be prepared? When would it be? These thoughts followed me into motherhood and became the source of some of my panic attacks following the traumatic birth of my second daughter.

In addition to being obsessed with my mortality, I had to worry about Sasha and Natalie because I was now responsible for raising them. Sasha was 16 and Natalie was 11 and boy, did those two give me a run for my money. I like to say that raising two crazy teenagers more than prepared me for whatever my own two girls throw at me when they hit that stage! But it also made my stress and anxiety levels rise. Would my sisters be alright? How would they cope with the loss of both our mother and father in a year and a half time frame? It didn't matter how I would cope. My thoughts and feelings came secondary to theirs.

My role switched from sister and confidant to sister-momma overnight. I did not have healthy methods of coping and neither did they. How could we when we were all products of dysfunction and never talking about your problems? I coped by working by day, binge drinking by night, and hopping in and out of dysfunctional relationships. This cycle continued for several years until I made Jesus

19

TJ Ogunlusi

Lord of my life in 2015. It was not until then that I began to really dig in and seek therapy for my issues.

Jesus

By 2014, I had grown tired of the cycle of going to work, binge drinking, and relationship hopping. By my own definition, I was having "fun," but something was missing. There was a void that drinking and sleeping with men just could not fill. Eventually, I realized that the missing puzzle piece was an intimate relationship with God. It was something that I yearned for.

Now, I had grown up in the church, but I had no idea of what a true relationship with God looked like. When we first moved to North Carolina, we attended the AME church that my great grandmother formerly attended. I remember being baptized for the first time with water being sprinkled on my forehead at that church. I had no idea what I was doing or why I was doing it, and I certainly did not feel any different afterwards.

My second baptism occurred after my family moved to Bladenboro, North Carolina. We began attending a Baptist church at that time. Unlike the previous church, we did have some education prior to being baptized. My entire family went through a weekly educational course that taught the "rules" of the church. We did not learn the biblical basis for baptism, nor did we learn why we were making the decision to be baptized other than to become members of the church. Though I was fully submerged in the water this time, I still walked away feeling exactly the same as before I got baptized.

The third time was the charm for me. After church hopping in my area and not finding anything that was a good fit, one of my best friends from college reached out to me to invite me to her small group Bible Talk with The Path Church (formerly known as the Greater Atlanta Church of Christ). Janee knew that I was looking for a church home and, most importantly, to build a relationship with God. Her Bible Talk group met on Thursday evenings inside of Target at Edgewood Plaza. That worked for me because I was able to attend the discussion and head over to Janee's place to watch How To Get Away With Murder since she lived right next door. One of the things that stood out to me was how welcoming everyone was and how I actually understood what was being discussed. There was no whooping and hollering, stomping, and sweating. There were biblical discussions with scriptures to back everything up, and I loved it. So, when Janee asked me if I wanted to study the Bible I was down. What was missing in my past church experiences was a true teaching and understanding of the Bible. I walked away from service each time not understanding a word the preacher said, and I certainly did not understand the King James Version (KJV) of the Bible. I didn't even know that there were different translations of the Bible until I began studying.

Sitting down and studying the Bible with a group of like-minded women was refreshing. I got the opportunity to learn about who Jesus is, the sacrifice he made on the Cross for me, how my personal sins helped to put Jesus on the Cross, and what it would take to be a true follower of Jesus. Throughout that six month time period, I learned so much about who my Father is and my own character. I knew that baptism was what I wanted because the Bible is clear about that, along with professing that Jesus is Lord being key to receiving salvation: "When the people heard this, they were cut to the heart and said to Peter and the other apostles, 'Brothers, what shall we do?' Peter replied, 'Repent and be baptized, every one of you, in the name of Jesus Christ for the forgiveness of your sins. And you will receive the gift of the Holy Spirit'" (2 Acts 2:37-38 NIV).

Even though I knew what needed to be done and wanted my heart to be there, it just wasn't quite yet. I was in an unequally yoked dating relationship at the time and did not take kindly to hearing it. None of the ladies told me what to do by any means. They simply showed me the scriptures, and I did not like it. I remember them sharing a scripture about the dangers of being unequally yoked: "Do not be yoked together with unbelievers. For what do righteousness and wickedness have in common? Or what fellowship can light have with darkness?" (2 Corinthians 6:14, NIV). Again, no one had told me that I needed to break up with this man. In fact, he was studying the Bible with a group of men himself and would later be baptized to become a Disciple of Jesus Christ. However, I was very convicted by the scripture, and it was the Holy Spirit nudging me to make a very tough decision. But I still wasn't ready. My head wanted to make Jesus Lord, but my heart was not ready. It would not click until I got to the root of why my heart was not in the right place. One day, during my study about the church, I broke down in tears. It had nothing to do with the content of this particular Bible study. It had finally clicked. The reason my heart was not in the right place was because I was still angry with God for taking my parents away. I still carried the bitter roots of pain, anger, and resentment and had never dealt with those feelings in a healthy way. And I had to wrestle that out with God. Once I jumped over that hurdle, it was time to learn what it truly meant to live in the light.

"But you are a chosen people, a royal priesthood, a holy nation, God's special possession, that you may declare the praises of him who called you out of darkness into his wonderful light" (1 Peter 2:9, NIV). It took me six months to realize that I was in the dark. Prior to this, I had thought of myself as a pretty good person, but because of my lifestyle, (I was alllll the way ratchet if I'm being completely honest) and the fact that God was not number one in my life, I was not in the light. When I finally realized where I was spiritually at the time, I broke down crying. I cried because it had finally clicked for me that MY sins had put Jesus on the Cross. My heart was finally in the same place as my head. I remember crying out to God about how I did not want to be in the dark anymore. I just wanted to be close to him, and I was willing to do whatever it took to get there. That included getting out of that unequally yoked relationship. I contacted my boyfriend at the time and let him know that I was breaking up with him. It was an extremely hard decision because I loved him. But at that point, I loved God more and had to do what it took to get right with Him. I then contacted my best friend Janee and told her that I was ready to be baptized. We scheduled my baptism for March 9, 2015.

I met with the ladies a few hours before my baptism to count the cost. It was important that I fully understood what it meant to pick up my cross daily and follow Jesus: "...Whoever wants to be my disciple must deny themselves and take up their cross daily and follow me. For whoever wants to save their life will lose it, but whoever loses their life for me will save it" (Luke 9:23-24, NIV). I was finally ready to take the plunge. With my friends and family as witnesses, I publicly professed that Jesus is Lord and was baptized and received the gift of the Holy Spirit. My sins were washed away and forgiven. I remember feeling fresh and new. I was reborn. My walk with Christ had begun.

One of the misconceptions I had when I was first baptized was that my life would always be easy as a Christian. I had experienced so much trauma prior to making Jesus Lord. Surely things could only go up from there. I now had an intimate relationship with God! Good things happen to good people, right? A relationship with God meant a life full of peace and prosperity at all times, right? No pain and suffering, right? Wrong. My mental health issues did not magically disappear just because I had made Jesus Lord. Yes, I had a relationship with God, but I would soon realize that there was no such thing as praying my mental health issues away. That is when I began my journey of seeking out a therapist.

Therapy

When I went to court to gain custody of Sasha and Natalie after my parents passed away, one of the things that the judge presiding over the case said to me was that we all needed to attend therapy. I verbally agreed with her, but in the back of my mind I was not here for it at all. We grew up in a household where we did not talk about our feelings. You felt whatever you were feeling in your bedroom alone. You cried alone, picked yourself back up, and came out of your room pretending nothing had ever happened. For me, that meant hiding the mental and physical scars that I had accumulated over the years.

Sometime in 2017, I had had enough. It had been six years since my dad had passed and four since my mom had passed, and I was in so much pain. There were days and nights when I felt like I was drowning. I had so many thoughts and feelings surrounding both deaths. With my dad, it was the idea that somehow it was my fault that he had died of an overdose because I had decided to go to college. With my mom, it was the fact that she was 39 years old when she was diagnosed with lung cancer and had been given only six months to live. I watched her deteriorate from the moment she was diagnosed and finally succumb to the illness a month later. I stuffed my feelings because I believed that I had no right to feel them. What right did I have to grieve when my sisters were 11 and 16 when this happened? I had to hold it together for them. But the load I carried was too much. I cried out to God and the pain just would not go away. After a certain point, I realized that it was time to talk to a professional. That was the only way that I would be able to begin the process of healing.

So, I began my Google search for therapists near me. At first, I did not have much of a criteria. This was my first time attending therapy, and I didn't know what to look for or what to expect. I just wanted someone who was close by. It didn't even matter if he/she looked like me. I ended up settling on a practice nearby and had my first appointment. Things went well enough for the first session. My therapist asked a lot of questions and at the end of the appointment, she made her diagnosis. She diagnosed me with General Anxiety Disorder and moderate depression. We continued to meet for a few months, and I got to work through some of the surface level grief I was feeling and thought that I was good to go. So, I decided to end the meetings, especially after my therapist changed offices and the location was no longer convenient for me.

I was fine for a little while, but in 2018 I found myself in a dark place. So many wonderful things had happened that year. I got married to my best friend and had some of the greatest students a teacher could ever ask for. I was promoted as Gifted Lead teacher at my school, and my department was over prom that year. I really enjoyed the extra responsibility and having people trust me as a leader. However, an incident at my school shattered all of that for me.

I was responsible for collecting funds for prom tickets during the school day. When you collect funds, you are to deposit them in the school safe immediately. However, my planning period was not until 5th period, so I would at least have to wait until my lunch break to run to the office to deposit the funds. I decided to keep them inside of my desk. Teachers were required to stand in the hallway between transitions. Sometime during the transition between 3rd and 4th period that day, a student went into my desk and took almost $1,000 worth of ticket funds. I was mortified. How could this happen, and on my watch?! I was hurt that a student (I never found out who it was) would go into my desk and steal, especially because I loved and trusted that group with all of my heart.

I was terrified because nothing like this had happened to me in all of my years of teaching and an investigation into what happened to the money had to be conducted. I understood that, of course, but I couldn't help but feel like people thought that I had something to do with it. I was told that the administration would have my back during the investigation, and they did for the most part. They sat with me while I was questioned by the district, but I believe that it was only done because they did not want to lose me as a teacher. Up until that point, I had tried to resign and move to another district multiple times and was always convinced to stay. However, something about being blamed for the money going missing did not sit well with me. Sure, I was eventually cleared of any wrongdoing and was just given a warning for not turning in the funds immediately upon receiving them. But, that was after I had an offer in a new district rescinded because of a pending ethics case against me surrounding the stolen money.

Though I was cleared of any wrongdoing, my heart was bitter. I began to hate many of the people at the school. That summer, the root of hatred eventually turned into depression. I put on a happy face, but I felt dead inside. I would go into the bathroom where nobody could see me and cry on the floor. I was so heartbroken about what had happened during that school year, and I was also struggling with being a newlywed. I had no idea who I was anymore. It was like I was having an existential crisis. Did my voice matter at work? Did it matter at home? What did it mean to submit? Would my friendships change as a result of me now being married? Why did God take my parents away and why during such a critical part of my life? There were so many thoughts and questions that flooded through my mind. God felt distant again.

My mental state was now having a negative impact on my relationship with God. It was time to seek out a therapist again. However, this time I knew what I wanted. Because I was struggling in my relationship with God, I wanted a therapist who was a Christian. I began doing research and stumbled upon Safe Harbor Christian Counseling. This new therapist was about ten minutes from my home, a Christian, and was also an African American woman married to a Nigerian man. This was significant because I too was an African American woman married to a Nigerian man, and cultural differences were a point of contention at different points in our marriage. It seemed like a perfect fit and after that first meeting, I knew that this was someone I could see long term. I began seeing her in July 2018. She, too, diagnosed me with General Anxiety Disorder and Moderate Depression. We began to untangle the web of trauma that I had never fully dealt with head on. I was able to get open about the guilt I felt about my dad's death. I was able to get open about wondering if his overdose was actually accidental or if he had committed suicide. I was able to get open about the fact that I never got to grieve my mother properly. And the best part of all was that this therapist always found a way to tie in my faith. She always found a way to point me back to the scriptures. I did not get that from my previous therapist and did not know that I needed it until I interacted with her.

One of the biggest "aha" moments that I had with a therapist occurred during my stay at a mental institution in December 2019. I'll discuss this more in detail later, but she helped me to uncover a traumatic event that occurred in graduate school and make the connection that my body had remembered this trauma despite me trying to stuff it deep down and suppress the memory. The process of finding the right therapist taught me that therapists are not one size fits all. I needed to see the first therapist in order to get accustomed to attending therapy regularly, but also to learn what I did not want in a therapist. I certainly did not want someone who would curse and quote scriptures in the same sentence. I wanted someone who was a Christian and could point me back to the Cross. Someone who knew the importance of having a relationship with God and seeing a therapist when necessary. Someone who understood the culture clash issues that would come up in my marriage. It was clear that this therapist was sent by God and was a perfect fit. However, I would soon find out that Jesus and therapy would not suffice for the level of mental health challenges that were yet to come.

Meds

As I mentioned before, many members of my immediate family were on medication for the mental health issues they struggled with, and I grew up thinking that taking medication meant that you were crazy. I was also hesitant to take any medication after my father passed. I had a fear of becoming addicted to meds because addiction is hereditary. But after I had my youngest daughter in August 2019, I had no choice but to accept the fact that I needed medication and that it did not make me any less of a Christian, or person for that matter.

My birth story was an interesting one to say the least. It began on July 3, 2019 when I went into pre-term labor. I called my OBGYN because I had experienced some intense itching all over my body. My doctor advised me to come in at 10:00 a.m. and after showering, I headed that way. I felt that it was a routine visit to double check that everything was going fine with my baby and was not worried. Once I got to the doctor, I had blood drawn to test my bile levels and was advised that I would be given a prescription just in case the tests determined that I had Cholestasis. Next, tests were done to check on the baby to see how she was doing. She was not responding on the ultrasound so I was placed on a machine and told that the baby would be monitored for 20 minutes to make sure everything was alright. I ended up being on the machine for 2 hours before being sent to the hospital for 24 hour monitoring. Though I was not concerned before this point, the fear kicked in because I was worried about my baby. I had also never been admitted to the hospital before, so this was an entirely new experience for me.

Once I arrived at the hospital, I was hooked up to machines for monitoring. It was after my arrival that the doctors realized that I was in preterm labor. The contractions were jumping around all over the screen. The crazy thing was that I did not feel a thing. Also, I was only 31 weeks pregnant at the time, and I was terrified because I was not fully prepared to give birth.

At that point, the chaos began. I was stuck with needles that had steroids in them to mature my daughter's lungs just in case I gave birth that day. I was also given magnesium and had a catheter painfully inserted because magnesium increases the risk of falls. The doctors wanted to prevent this, so I was not allowed to leave the bed to use the restroom or shower. I was told that I would be at the hospital for a minimum of 72 hours. I had no idea how much time had passed, but it felt like it was a matter of minutes. Once my husband and friends arrived at the hospital, I felt relieved to not be alone. The doctors were able to stop the labor and at this point, it was a matter of monitoring me to make sure that I did not go back into labor. The next few days were pretty uneventful with the exception of having some amazing friends from church visit me and my family to keep us company during the stay. During that tough time, I was able to see God's love through His people and it renewed my faith.

I was eventually discharged after being told that I was on strict bed rest until I was full term. I remember being upset and feeling like my life was disrupted. My birthday trip was planned for that coming weekend, and I had work training to attend the next week. All of that was put on hold and I struggled. Those who know me best know that I do not like to sit down. I am always on the go. To be told that I was now put on bedrest was horrible news. However, God had made it clear that it was time to sit my behind down and allow people to help me.

My church came through for me and my family during this difficult time. They set up a meal train and brought meals to us weekly. They warned me that I better stay in bed and not do too much. They visited just to spend time with me. On my birthday, my best friends, Niya and Janee, brought me my favorite foods and two dear friends came to perform the song that my husband and I danced to for our first dance at our wedding. Everyone was so thoughtful that it was hard not to be grateful. However, I was still counting down the days until I would be full term and could resume business as usual.

Once I was 37 weeks, my doctor started talking to me about an induction and said that since I was Group B Strep positive, it was critical that I receive antibiotics in time to protect my baby. I did not trust that because I was so against being induced, so I got other opinions. I spoke to my doula, who said that induction was not necessary. My husband and I had built a relationship with her, so we trusted her judgment. However, the doctors continued to pressure me. I felt like my choice did not matter and that I was not heard. At 38 weeks 4 days, I went back to my OBGYN and was sent to the hospital because I was 6 cm dilated, which is considered active labor. At this point, I was so over being pregnant. It is not easy waddling around with a baby in your stomach in August. That Georgia heat is no joke! I was scared and excited because it was finally time to push my baby out!

Once I got to the hospital, things progressed very slowly, so the doctors decided that they would give me a low dose of Pitocin to make my labor progress more quickly. However, doctors kept increasing the Pitocin, sometimes on their own accord. I felt they knew what they were doing, but after they increased the medication without my input, I started to question their motives. Several hours later, things picked up because my water was broken. Once I was 8 cm, my labor progressed quickly and painfully. I remember being in so much pain and feeling so hot that I ripped the hospital gown off. Once it was time to push, I was terrified. My birth experience with my first daughter resulted in hemorrhaging, and I was so afraid that it would happen again. I recall telling the doctors and midwife that I was so scared. My doula, husband, and mother-in-law reassured me that I could do it, and so I did.

Trinity was born at 1:45 a.m. on August 24, 2019. She was very alert when she was born, barely crying and looking all around the room. This was a preview of the alert and rambunctious little girl she would grow into. I attempted to do skin to skin with her. However, she was barely on me for a few seconds before she was whisked away and handed to my husband. That is when the chaos really began. I was severely hemorrhaging, so the doctors tried several painful techniques to try to stop the bleeding. I was exhausted and asked them to leave me alone and one of the doctors or midwives responded by saying that they were trying to stop me from bleeding to death. I remember those words clearly. At this point, I was still exhausted. I had a similar experience with the birth of Tamara and did not realize that this situation was more serious. I thought it would play out the same way with the doctors pulling out the extra placenta and stopping the bleeding.

I was given fentanyl and handed a consent form to sign while I was high on the meds. I was so out of it that I did not feel fear or any emotion at that point. While the doctors were working on me, my husband's questions went unanswered. I was told that I had to have a procedure done to get the bleeding to stop but that I would not be put to sleep. That was critical to me. I did not want to be put to sleep, so I felt reassured when the doctors told me that I would not be. However, that was not true because I did end up being put under. I was in the birthing room for a while before being moved to the room where the procedure was to be done. I remember everyone being asked to leave; I was alone again. It did not bother me then, but it bothers me now. I later developed a fear of bad things happening to me when I am alone.

There was still some waiting before the procedure began, and then I remember the anesthesiologist saying that they were going to put me to sleep. I felt lied to. Later on, I realized how angry I was. I felt that I had been misled and it reminded me of when my mother was sick with cancer and the doctor called to tell me that she had six months left to live. Because she passed shortly after that, I felt like I was lied to. Also, she had been to the doctor several times prior to her cancer diagnosis and was told on numerous occasions that it was just bronchitis.

This contributed to my overall mistrust for doctors. The strong feeling that they are untrustworthy liars comes and goes. While I did not realize that these events had an impact on me in those moments, they began to affect me months later. In November 2019, I started having panic attacks. There were specific things about the birth room, such as the dim lights and the shape of the lights, that would trigger the panic attacks if I found myself in a room with a similar setting. The bright fluorescent lights in the operating room also affected me. I remember having panic attacks later when in similar lighting situations. Perhaps the most significant part of the experience that impacted me the most was waking up right after the procedure. I remember being told to breathe into a mask and the next thing I knew, I was waking up in a different room with severe throat pain. It took me a while to figure out where I was and what had happened. I was confused about why my throat was hurting so badly and I was told about things that had been done to me while I was out, including blood transfusions. I was getting bits and pieces of information about what had happened to me during the procedure and that was frustrating.

Later these feelings would turn into feelings of violation. While I did not feel violated in the exact moments after the procedure, the feelings of violation became very intense later. Many of my panic attacks would occur when I suddenly woke up out of my sleep and did not know where I was. This was because of the confusion I felt right after the procedure. But, the specific feelings of violation occurred because I made a connection between the doctors being inside of me during the procedure and the sexual assault and violation I experienced as a student in graduate school. During my second year in graduate school, I was sexually assaulted by a guy who I was talking to at the time. We had gotten into an argument because he had slept with someone else. In order to "pacify" me, he pushed me face down onto the bed and assaulted me. I remember laying there and just taking it and questioning whether or not I was really raped. After all, this was a guy I had been intimate with before. This was a guy who I let into my room. I blamed myself and so I never said anything until December 2019. A therapist in the treatment facility I was in began questioning why I felt so violated by the doctors and if I had ever been raped. I had been, and I finally said the words out loud that day.

So many things now began to make sense. Why I would cry during moments of intimacy with my husband. Why I would react with anger when he wanted to have sex and I did not. One time, I was so enraged that I stormed into the bathroom and began tearing things up. I tore down the shower curtain and threw things around. I was livid because I felt pressure. As a disclaimer, my husband never violated me in any way. But being raped had a negative impact on our intimacy and because my husband was not made privy to that information until early 2020, there was no way that he could know why I was reacting with so much anger.

So, every time I imagined the doctors inside of me with their tools while I was sleeping, I would feel an intense anger that this had happened to me and spent a lot of time just crying about that alone. The thought made me livid. I did not understand why until later, but I knew I was livid that they had the audacity to do these things to me without my consent. It took a while for me to separate that experience from what I experienced in grad school. I am still working on that.

I felt anger for so many other reasons as well. I felt that I had done all of these things to prepare for Trinity's birth and ensure that my birth experience was a smooth one. When things did not go according to plan, I felt so much guilt, as if I had not done enough to make things run smoothly and that I should have done more, including advocating for myself throughout labor. I felt like I had not advocated for myself in the labor and delivery room, just like I did not speak up in that dorm room and for years to come.

My panic attacks intensified after I was diagnosed with postpartum preeclampsia. After being told that

43

my blood pressure was at stroke levels and being sent to the hospital during my 6 week checkup, I became paranoid and obsessed about my blood pressure and overall health. I was afraid of dying. I would check my blood pressure several times a day even though I was told by my PCP to check it once every other day. I became paranoid that I would have a stroke or heart attack at any moment. I would go to Google with every random symptom I felt and diagnose myself with deadly diseases. Even after I came off of blood pressure medication, I did not trust the doctors. I continued to obsess and check my blood pressure constantly. I forced my husband to take me to the hospital and if he didn't, I would call 911 and get them to take me. I had convinced myself that I would drop dead at any moment. I was still seeing my therapist and even began seeing a therapist who deals with postpartum mood disorders, but this was not enough. It was time for medication.

After being diagnosed with PTSD and Panic Disorder, I ended up taking a medical leave of absence from work and setting up an appointment with a psychiatrist. He put me on Zoloft and said that the only side effect I would experience was a loss of libido. I was fine with that. I just wanted the panic attacks to stop. However, nobody warned me about other side effects. When people who suffer with panic attacks take antidepressants, there can be a couple of weeks of increased anxiety. Nobody warned me about that. I thought that I was crazy and kept running back and forth to the emergency room. Because I was now having heart palpitations as a symptom of my panic attacks, I could not tell if I was having a panic attack or dying of a heart attack. This was happening 3-4 times a week, which led me to sink into a deep, dark depression.

If you remember, I was diagnosed with depression before, but it was always a moderate form of depression. This was different. This was the darkest and lowest I had ever felt in my life. I could not even pick myself off of the floor to take a shower. I got to a point where I no longer wanted to live if living meant I would continue to have panic attacks and have a constant fear of dying. I could not function. I wanted to die.

Around Christmas 2019, it was like I snapped. I had taken Klonopin, a benzodiazepine that treats the acute symptoms of panic. However, nobody warned me that these medications can sometimes cause suicidal ideation. I remember grabbing a knife and locking myself in a room. I began scratching myself with the knife and contemplating how to kill myself. I began googling ways to kill myself. My husband was able to bust into the room and take the knife from me, but that did not stop the feelings of me wanting to die.

The next day, I had a nervous breakdown and called my therapist. Once I told her that I had been googling ways to kill myself, she told me to call 911 immediately. This resulted in me being committed to a mental institution for 6 days. While there, my dose of Zoloft was increased to 100mg. Once I was stable enough to be released, it was mandatory for me to see both my therapist and my psychiatrist. I began seeing my main therapist weekly and was set up with my postpartum therapist weekly as well. Both therapists communicated with one another and came up with a Cognitive Behavioral Treatment (CBT) plan to help me heal. However, my meds were still not right. Neither was my psychiatrist.

My physical symptoms of anxiety were not getting better, so I talked to my psychiatrist about changing to Lexapro, another SSRI (selective serotonin reuptake inhibitor) used to treat anxiety. He was against it despite me telling him that my medication was not working and my therapist backing me up. I knew that it was time to find someone else. However, that was tough because most psychiatrists stay booked months out. I was eventually able to schedule an appointment with a psychiatrist through LiveHealth. What stood out to me the most about my new psychiatrist was the fact that he listened to me and tailored my treatment plan to fit my needs. He tapered me off of Zoloft and started me on Lexapro. He warned me of side effects and stayed in contact with me through all dose increases and the uncomfortable side effects. He took his time to work with me until my dose of Lexapro was just right. Unfortunately, I ended up having to switch to a new psychiatrist for insurance purposes. However, I only have to see her once a month to make sure that my medication is still working and so far, it is. My panic attacks have stopped. I only experience anxiety the week before my period is coming or when I am over-whelmed. Despite my initial apprehension, medication was the final piece of my healing puzzle.

Jesus, Therapy, and Meds: The Trifecta

I have learned so much about myself during this healing journey. I learned about some deeply rooted fears that I did not realize I have. I learned that I have the strength to take my thoughts captive: "We demolish arguments and every pretension that sets itself up against the knowledge of God, and we take captive every thought to make it obedient to Christ" (2 Corinthians 10:5, NIV). I have learned my limits and how to set boundaries. I have learned that it is okay to say no. I learned that I am healthy and that my birth experience was not necessarily a bad experience. It was an experience. I learned to face my triggers and fears head on. I learned that contrary to popular belief, you cannot just pray your mental health issues away and that there is nothing wrong with taking medication. I learned that I have been advocating for myself all along. I learned that I do not have to look over my shoulder or live in fear. I can actually enjoy life and live it to the fullest.

I learned that healing is not linear. Let me repeat that. Healing is not linear. I am in a better place today than I have ever been in my entire life. However, this is not the end of my story. I am still healing. I still have a relationship with God. I still see my therapist. I still take my medication. And I am unapologetic about it.

I remember sitting in a moms' support group a few months ago and hearing a mother say that she was suffering from postpartum depression but did not want to have to resort to taking medication. I was already on medication at this point, so of course, I felt some type of way. There is such a stigma around taking medication for mental health issues. But those meds literally saved my life. If I had not sought help, talked to other moms who have gone through their own mental health challenges, and advocated for my meds to be right for me, I would not be here today and you might have been reading an obituary rather than this memoir. Though it may not seem possible while you are in the midst of your storm, remember that you will come out on the other side and be a stronger person because of it. Read your Bible. Talk to God. Go to therapy. And take those meds if you need to. You got this. #JesusTherapyandMeds

Best Practices for an Effective Trifecta

On the next few pages, I'll share my best practices for creating your own effective trifecta of #Jesus-TherapyandMeds. My reason for sharing these best practices is because several people shared with me. This memoir is not just about my personal experiences but the collective experiences of the many people who played integral roles in my healing journey. It is my hope that any of my readers who are going through a tough time, or know someone who is going through a tough time, can use the best practices as a starting point to getting the help you need.

#Jesus

Get connected and STAY connected!

I cannot stress how important it is to have a church HOME. I church hopped for a while, and I am grateful that I was able to get connected to The Path Church. Having a body of believers who knew what was happening with me and could intercede and pray on my behalf was an absolute necessity. I'll never forget the Sunday that I had a panic attack at the welcome table at church. Or the Sunday I had a panic attack during our Medical Day service because the white coats triggered me. Both times, sisters came and comforted me with prayer and scriptures.

They let me know that it was okay to feel what I was feeling. It was okay if I needed to step out of service to take a breather. There was absolutely nothing wrong with me needing to take a break. Though the temptation to withdraw and disconnect may be strong, staying connected to the vine is critical, especially during tough seasons in life.

Have your go-to Scriptures on DECK!

Write them on sticky notes, notecards, commit them to memory, tattoo them on your skin (I did)...do whatever you need to do because you will need them as a reminder of who God is. Satan is going to convince you that you are nothing and you will need to be able to combat those lies with God's truth! Some of my go-to scriptures during this season are listed below. I encourage you to find some favorites of your own so that you can hold on to them during the valleys of life.

Isaiah 41:10: So do not fear, for I am with you; do not be dismayed, for I am your God. I will strengthen you and help you; I will uphold you with my righteous hand (NIV)

Jeremiah 29:11-13: "For I know the plans I have for you," declares the Lord, "plans to prosper you and not harm you, plans to give you hope and a future. Then you will call on me and come and pray to me, and I will listen to you. You will seek me and find me when you seek me with all your heart (NIV)

Romans 8:28: And we know that in all things God works for the good of those who love him, who have been called according to his purpose (NIV)

Cry Out to God!

I'm not going to lie to you. My prayer life has been a rollercoaster during this healing journey. At the beginning, I was so faithful. I was praying everywhere. I just knew that I would be healed in a few weeks. When the panic attacks kept coming, my faith would begin to dwindle. Those prayers turned into cries of despair. I could not understand why this was happening to me. My prayer life was a cycle. Praise God. Stop praying completely. Scream and cry. Journal. Repeat. God wants to hear from us. He wants to hear our cries. Don't hold back. Hold 1 Thessalonians 5:16-17 close to your heart: Rejoice always, pray continually, give thanks in all circumstances; for this is God's will for you in Christ Jesus. (NIV)

Have a Spiritual SQUAD!

Simply put, we need sound spiritual friendships in order to make it into Heaven. We need a spiritual squad to be successful on our walk. By squad, I mean people who know the good, bad, and downright dirty ugly stuff about you, and you know the same about them. These are people who do not judge you. Instead, they point you back to the Cross by sharing scriptures and praying with and for you. They tell you when you're tripping. I am grateful that I had a spiritual squad prior to entering this tough season. Janee, Tina, Niya, Kenya, and Kristen were there for me before, during, and now as I am continuing on this journey. But I also got blessed with another group of women who were added to my spiritual squad: Melissa, Andrea, Carina, and Christina. I am so blessed to be part of a Bible Talk with women in the same season of life as me, some of whom have also endured mental health challenges of their own. It is so refreshing to have these nine spiritual queens in my life. I do not know where I would be without them. Ladies and Gentlemen, get yourself a squad if you do not have one already.

#Therapy

What I have learned is that a great therapist is not one size fits all. A therapist who comes highly recommended by one person may not necessarily be the best fit for you. Here are some tips for finding the right therapist.

Have an Idea of What You are Looking For!

Like I said before, I had no idea what the heck I was looking for when I first started going to therapy. However, after the first experience, I made my mental list. I wanted someone who was Black, a wife and/or mom, and most importantly, a Christian. It was an added bonus that she was married to a Nigerian man. Trust me, God knew that I needed someone who would understand that aspect of my marriage. I was able to take my mental list, Google search, call around, and find the best therapist for me. My therapist and I are riding until the wheels fall off!

Know Your Budget!

If you have insurance, you should be able to call Member Services and get a list of therapists in your area who take your insurance. They can email you a list and you will be able to look up reviews and other pertinent information and set up an appointment at your convenience. If you do not have insurance, your county should have behavioral health services offered at a sliding scale. Hope Counseling Centers is one of the offices that offers those services for residents in the metro Atlanta area.

You May Need More Than One Therapist...That's Perfectly Okay!

My current therapist does not specialize in postpartum mood disorders. While I continued to see her, I needed something more when my PTSD was at its worst since a lot of it was connected to my birth experience. The Supported Mama offers an array of services for moms and moms to be, including therapy. Being able to work through my trauma with someone who was trained to treat it was amazing.

Talking to someone who understood what it's like being a mom to a newborn and the identity crisis that goes along with that was priceless. If you are experiencing mental health challenges that are a little more complex like mine were, do not be afraid to seek additional help.

#Meds

Meds, Meds, Meds...There are multiple classes of medications that treat a variety of mental health disorders, and it's critical to know when or even IF you need medication. Here are my suggestions if it is determined that you need medication.

You NEED a Psychiatrist!

There is no way around this. Yes, a PCP can prescribe medication. However, they rarely know how these medications work when it comes to side effects and psychiatrists are trained to manage psychiatric medications. My PCP is the first person who started me on Lexapro. However, she started me at too high of a dose and did not know what the side effects were. I took it once, had heart palpitations, and quit. Next, I was on Zoloft, then back on

Lexapro. If I had been warned about side effects up front, I would have known what to expect. I would have started at a lower dose and slowly tapered up. I would have known that SSRIs can increase anxiety the first few weeks if you are taking it for anxiety. I know, ironic right?! Long story short, you NEED a psychiatrist.

You Need the RIGHT Psychiatrist!

Just like therapists, psychiatrists are not one size fits all. I have gone through three. A psychiatrist is not a therapist, so your appointments may be pretty cut and dry. However, they should still listen to you. If you run into a situation like I did, where your needs are not being taken into consideration, find a new psychiatrist. Do not settle. Adjusting to a new medication is hard enough. You deserve a psychiatrist who listens and is supportive.

There Will Be Side Effects...and the Meds WILL Take Time to Work!

Make sure that you talk to your psychiatrist about possible side effects. Some medications have more than others and one person may experience a side effect that you may not. For instance, I experienced heart palpitations with Lexapro, but my friend did not. If I had known what side effects to expect and that they were TEMPORARY, I would have stuck with Lexapro and avoided the yo-yo between SSRIs. Also, it takes about six weeks for you to start seeing improvement and up to twelve to feel like yourself again. If after twelve weeks you are not feeling better, you may need to increase your dose or change your medication. Finding the right antidepressant is a process of trial and error and takes time. But, it is worth it. At least it was for me.

Resources

Finally, I want to leave you with some helpful resources if you should ever find yourself needing them:

1. Suicide Prevention Hotline: 1-800-273-8255 or Text GO to 741741

2. Postpartum Support International: 1-800-944-4773 or Text 503-894-9453 (English) 971-420-0294 (Spanish)

3. Georgia Behavioral Health Professionals: https://www.mygbhp.com/

4. Peer Support Wellness & Respite Centers: https://www.gmhcn.org/peer-support-wellness-respite

5. Virtual Monthly Mommy Meetups: www.realtalkidentity.com
6. Nugget to Newborn Mom Support Group (Facebook)
7. Physical Health and Wellness: www.fitmom-atl.com
8. Mommy Prayer Groups: www.momsin-prayer.org
9. Safe Harbor Christian Counseling (National): 1-800-305-2089
10. The Path Church: www.thepath.church

Acknowledgements

I would like to take this time to personally thank the village of people who have reminded me that I am more than a conqueror during my journey of healing: My loving husband Wande, Moji and Olu Ogunlusi, Mimi, Janee, Niya, Tina, Kenya, Kristen Carina, Alex, Hollie, Ariel, Tia, Risa, Daphne, Brunia, Christina, the women of The Clean Campaign, and all of the members of my church family at The Path Church. Thank you for reminding me that healing is not linear and to cling to God through whatever season I may find myself in. God's love shines through each and every one of you.

Connect
with the Author

Website: www.authortjogunlusi.com
Facebook: Author T. J. Ogunlusi
Instagram: @authortjogunlusi

Creative Control With Self-Publishing

Divine Legacy Publishing provides authors with the
guid-ance necessary to take creative control of their
work through self-publishing. We provide:

Writing Coaching

Professional Editing

Author Branding

Self-Publishing
Coaching

Graphic Design

Website Design

**Let Divine Legacy Publishing help you
master the business of self-publishing.**

Made in the USA
Columbia, SC
12 April 2021